NIKKI GRIMES

ANEESA LEE
and
the Weaver's Gift

ILLUSTRATED BY
ASHLEY BRYAN

LOTHROP, LEE AND SHEPARD BOOKS

NEW YORK

For Nancy Gary Ward,
whose wondrous weavings inspired me
NG

For Eva Brussels Mason
and Sara Weeks Peabody,
good friends for over fifty years
AB

Tempera and gouache paints were used for the full-color illustrations.
The text type is 13-point Raleigh.

Text copyright © 1999 by Nikki Grimes
Illustrations copyright © 1999 by Ashley Bryan

Published by Lothrop, Lee & Shepard Books
a division of William Morrow and Company, Inc.
1350 Avenue of the Americas, New York, NY 10019
www.williammorrow.com

Printed in the United States of America.

2 4 6 8 10 9 7 5 3 1

LIBRARY OF CONGRESS CATALOGING-IN-PUBLICATION DATA
is available upon request.
ISBN 0-688-15997-4 (trade)
ISBN 0-688-15998-2 (library)

WEAVING WORDS

Beater: a movable part of the loom used to evenly pack the widthwise (weft) threads together as they are woven through the lengthwise (warp) threads

Dressing the loom: the process of attaching the warp threads to the loom

Dyestuff: any substance used to color yarn; dye

Harness: a part of the loom that holds the warp threads and moves up or down to form the shed

Heddle: an eyelet used to attach a warp thread to the harness

Loom: a frame or machine used to weave yarn into cloth

Reed: a comblike device on the beater that keeps the warp threads evenly spaced when the weft threads are packed together

Shed: the openings made between the warp threads for the weft thread to weave through

Shuttle: a device that carries the weft thread through the shed, weaving over and under the warp threads

Spinning wheel: a machine used to spin yarn

Tapestry: a kind of cloth where the design is the same on both sides of the fabric

Thread: the yarn used to weave cloth

Treadle: a foot pedal

Yarn: a long string made by twisting together strands of shorter fibers

Warp: the threads that run the length of a piece of cloth

Warp beam: a beam on the loom used to store the warp

Warping board: a peg board used to sort different yarns to dress the loom

Weft: the threads that run the width of a piece of cloth

Yarn

Shuttle

Weft thread

Loom

Harness

Warp threads

Beater

Reed

Heddles

Warp beam

Treadles

THE WEAVER

Aneesa Lee would sooner weave than anything—
A scarf in winter or lacy shawl in spring,
A band of satin ribbon for her hair,
A belt of turquoise cotton cord to wear.

Aneesa softly hums and weaves away
The minutes and the hours of the day,
And rolls the cloth of time upon her loom
Till yards of night unfold inside her room.

ANEESA LEE

Aneesa,
like her mother,
is a weave
of black
and white
and Japanese
a blend that sometimes
led to teasing,
and yet these strands
produced a pleasing,
living, breathing tapestry
christened Aneesa Lee.

FAMILY GATHERING

Beneath the forest canopy
Aneesa and her family
Enjoy a Sunday's peaceful pleasure
Gathering blueberry treasure
And dining out on sweets.

Then all join in Aneesa's search
For maple, alder, and white birch,
For marigold and goldenrod,
Raw dyestuff sprouting from the sod.

All dandelions, roots, and nettles,
Berries and wildflower petals
Possess within at least a hint
Of Mother Nature's rainbow tint.

Aneesa works her spade and dreams
Of dipping silk in saffron pools,
And elderberry lilac streams,
Of wringing green from privet leaves,
And all the while her cuffs and sleeves
Are staining green and purple.

ANEESA AT THE WHEEL

Aneesa dances at the wheel.
She's seated, yes, but hardly still.
Her right foot tappity-taps the pedal,
Creating music on the treadle.
She reels out wispy clouds of cotton.

    Twist, twirl
    Twist, twirl

The spinning wheel whirls, all time forgotten
As, magically, once gossamer stuff
Becomes through her fingers sturdy enough
For weaving cloth that is sure to last
At least one hundred years.

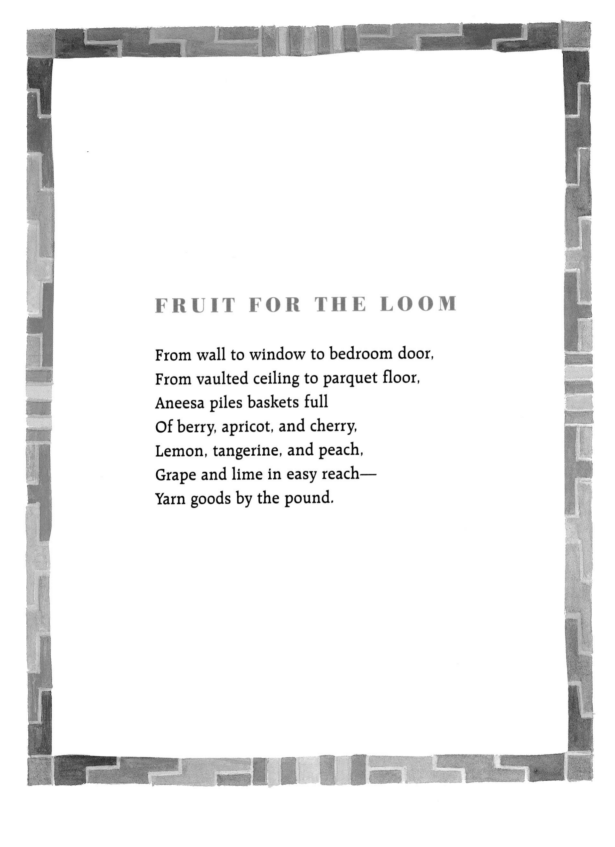

FRUIT FOR THE LOOM

From wall to window to bedroom door,
From vaulted ceiling to parquet floor,
Aneesa piles baskets full
Of berry, apricot, and cherry,
Lemon, tangerine, and peach,
Grape and lime in easy reach—
Yarn goods by the pound.

THE WARPING BOARD

Measuring unbroken lengths
Of yarn takes time,
And yet, Aneesa knows
The reason and the rhyme:

To wind yarn enough to make the cloth one plans,
One adds, subtracts, and multiplies the strands.

How closely will the fibers fit
Within the weave?
How large a space between them
Should she leave?
Each detail must be plotted
In advance,
Computed inch by inch,
Not left to chance.

Strokes of luck in weaving are too rare.
Far wiser, then, to plan ahead with care.

DRESSING THE LOOM

Before the sun, Aneesa rises
To quickly dress herself
And dress the loom
That crowds her tiny room.

Lips pursed tight, she delicately
Winds round the loom's warp beam
Yards of raw and polished silk
In shades of peach and cream.

She threads the silver heddles
Strand by single strand,
Guiding through each velvet strip
With sure and steady hand.

She threads the reed that combs
And holds each strand in place,
Then ties the dangling ends
In front where she finds space.

Aneesa sighs. The dressing's done.
No threads remain to spin,
No yarn to wrap or wind.
So now—at last!—the weaving can begin.

LOVE IS PURPLE

Love is purple velvet
with gold and turquoise fringe.

Confusion is a mohair fuzz,
a swirling, mud-brown tinge.

Jealousy is sharp jade nubs
and looping strands of green.

Loneliness is deeply shaded
wispy ultramarine.

Aneesa draws her feelings out
in blues and reds and mints.

Her yarns express her deepest thoughts
in variegated tints.

SUNSET

Thoughts of Grandma make Aneesa smile,
But sorrow's shadow hangs there all the while.
Aneesa weaves her sad and sweet remembering.

Through heddles, shed, and reed,
Joy and sadness blend.
The beater presses them together,
End to end.

Aneesa leaves her sorrow in the cloth
And, when her evening handiwork is done,
Glowing pink and coral from the loom,
Appears a woven square of setting sun.

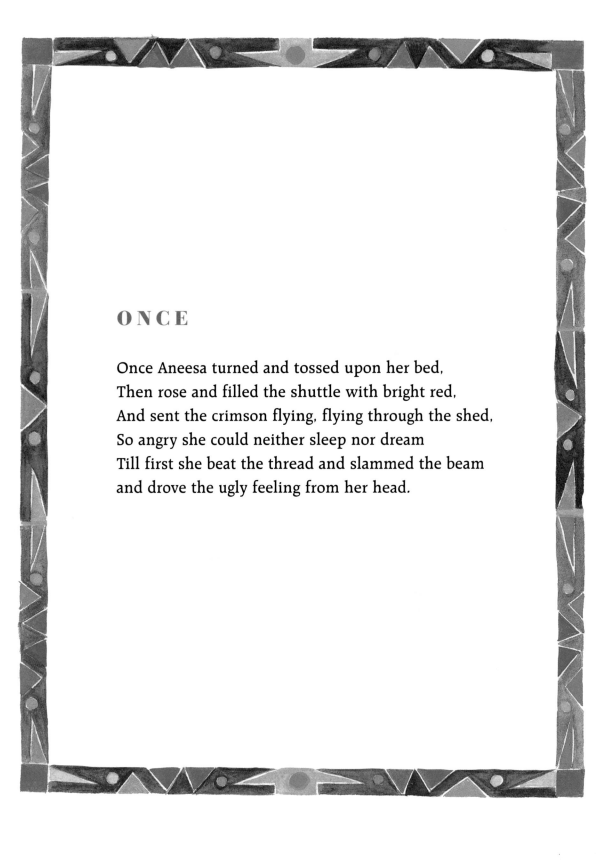

ONCE

Once Aneesa turned and tossed upon her bed,
Then rose and filled the shuttle with bright red,
And sent the crimson flying, flying through the shed,
So angry she could neither sleep nor dream
Till first she beat the thread and slammed the beam
and drove the ugly feeling from her head.

THE TAPESTRY

Aneesa rolls the cloth off the loom,
Revealing as the underside unfurls:

> a herringbone of sadness,
> > threads of anger and gladness;
> wispy hairs of hope,
> > bumpy rows of worry;
> feelings laced or knotted,
> > others smooth or furry;
> squares of hurt now sharing
> > stripes of love and caring.

Aneesa marvels at the way
The dangling threads behind can hide
The beauty of the fabric's other side!

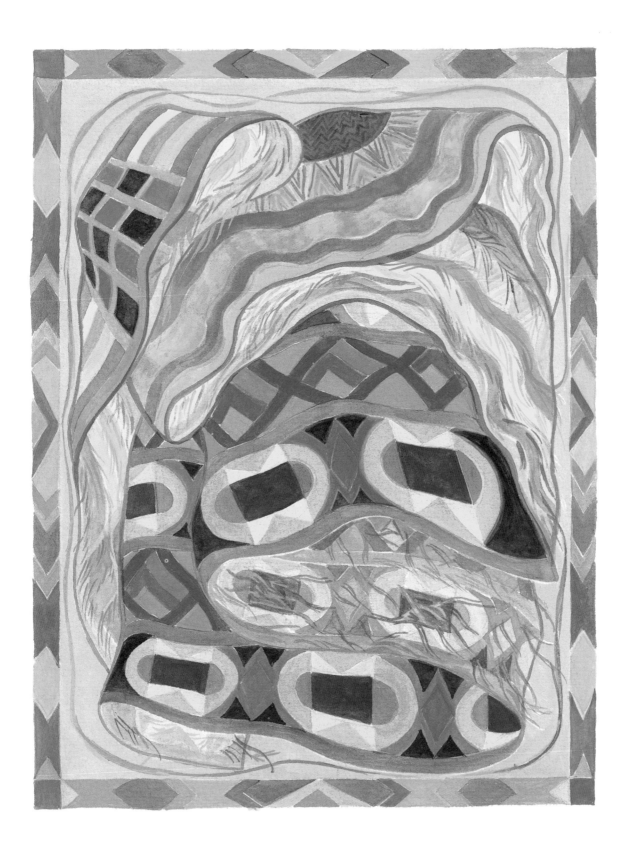

WHOLE CLOTH

Aneesa's family
loops around the table
holding hands,
fingers interlaced.
Love is the thread
that tightly binds them
at this hour,
in this place.

WEAVING A WORLD

From the age of bronze
To the age of space,
From Ankara to Zanzibar,
In every time, in every place,
Wherever thinking people are,
The weaver's craft is found.

For weaving is
A common joy,
A people's art
All peoples did and do—
In ancient times and new.

The loom connects us all
In a community
Of cloth.

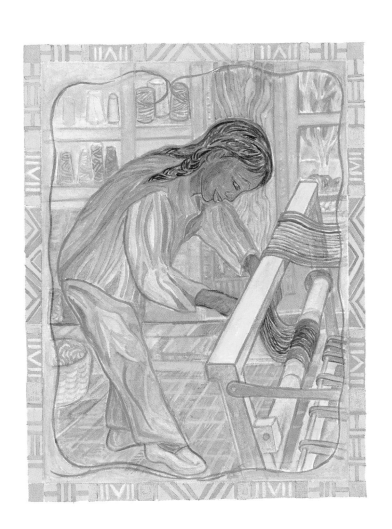